ducational Wooden Toys

Sri Lanka

im Godwin & Marjorie Wright

RACTICAL ACTION
blishing

Practical Action Publishing Ltd
27a Albert Street, Rugby, CV21 2SG,
Warwickshire, UK
www.practicalactionpublishing.org

© Intermediate Technology Publications 1984.

First published 1984\Digitised 2013

ISBN 10: 1 853390 53 4
ISBN 13: 9781853390531

Since 1974, Practical Action Publishing (formerly Intermediate Technology Publications
ITDG Publishing) has published and disseminated books and information in support
international development work throughout the world. Practical Action Publishing is a tra
name of Practical Action Publishing Ltd (Company Reg. No. 1159018), the wholly own
publishing company of Practical Action. Practical Action Publishing trades only in suppo
its parent charity objectives and any profits are covenanted back to Practical Action (Cha
Reg. No. 247257, Group VAT Registration No. 880 9924 76).

This case study was written by Marjorie Wright, based on trip reports by Tim Godwin.

Tim Godwin, the consultant for the Sri Lankan toy project, is an industrial designer who grew up in India and has had direct experience in setting up his own wooden toy firm in the UK.

Marjorie Wright, formerly a journalist, is a freelance writer whose work for Intermediate Technology Industrial Services includes the Project Bulletins, a series of information documents on ITIS project work.

i

ACKNOWLEDGMENTS

The toy programme in Sri Lanka on which this case study is based has received support from a number of contributors. The consultant would like to thank the following for their help and enthusiasm which has been instrumental to the project's success:

The participating members of the Sarvodaya Shramadana Movement and in particular Dr. A.T. Ariyaratne, President, Mrs. Rajasuriya, Vice President, Mrs. Jayasekera, Christy Jayakody, Mr. Tennakone, Mr. Seneviratne, the toy workshop Co-ordinator, and Elise Sadler, a volunteer working with Savodaya.

Philip Kgosana of UNICEF and Mrs. Dias of Sri Lanka (I.Y.C.) Secretariat for their insights and advice.

The Redd Barna Colombo staff for collaborating in the establishment of the Teacher Training Programme.

Oxfam UK for contributing additional funding during the implementation stage.

Sunil Wimaladhara and Patrick Amarasinghe, local entrepreneurs, for their helpful information and advice.

CONTENTS

Introduction – Meeting the Need v

CHAPTER I: SUMMARY OF THE PROJECT 1
    Feasibility Study. 1
    Implementation. 2

CHAPTER 2: TOY DESIGNS. 5

CHAPTER 3: SETTING UP PRODUCTION WORKSHOP . .9
    Layout and Equipment. 9
    Raw Materials and Consumables 12
    Staff and Training. 14

CHAPTER 4: TOY PRODUCTION. 17

CHAPTER 5: MARKETS AND MARKETING 21
    Internal Sales. 21
    Home Market 21
    Export. 23

CHAPTER 6: FINANCIAL CONSIDERATIONS 26
    Capital Costs. 26
    Production Costs. 26
    Projections and Profitability 27

CHAPTER 7: THE PRE-SCHOOL TEACHER TRAINING
    PROGRAMME 28
    Programme Outline. 28
    Toy Evaluation 29
    Making Toys from Scrap. 30

CHAPTER 8: SIX MONTHS ON – A FOLLOW UP VISIT.31
    Marketing and Further Sales 34

CHAPTER 9: REPLICATION. 36

APPENDICES 39

FOREWORD

Dr. A.T. Ariyarante is President of the Sarvodaya Shramadana Movement, the Sri Lankan development charity which collaborated with Intermediate Technology Industrial Services in establishing the Educational Wooden Toy Project.

> *The Sarvodaya Pre-School Programme was started to satisfy a very vital need which was missing in our society for many years. This was the scarcity of educational institutions for the children of pre-school age. The few Montessori schools established in urban areas were only for the rich elite, and the poor children of the rural areas were neglected and deprived of this education.*
>
> *It was in this context that the emergence of a network of Sarvodaya pre-schools took place and this was geared to prepare these children for their formal education and to socialise them, as well as to meet their nutritional and health care needs.*
>
> *Due to the lack of funds on the part of the Movement, these pre-schools could not be provided with sufficient materials. Therefore, when the ITIS established its toy workshop at Moratuwa, it proved to be a great solace to these children. Our primary concern, now, is to provice all Sarvodaya Children's Service Centres in the island with these toys.*
>
> *I would particularly like to thank Tim Godwin for his hard work and enthusiasm in setting up the ITIS/Sarvodaya toy programme.*
>
> *It is also my hope that this case study will encourage other organisations to provide similar advantages to children in their own countries.*

> *Dr. A.T. Ariyaratne,*
> *Moratuwa*
> *Sri Lanka*
> *December, 1983*

INTRODUCTION – MEETING THE NEED

The value of early learning through play is an established concept in the industrialised world yet the potential benefits of educational play materials for developing countries are largely ignored.

In most of the Third World, the availability of educational toys – toys designed to aid in the formation of intellectual and practical skills – is limited to imports. These are scarce, expensive and reach only a privileged few.

Ironically, in those countries where local toy production *is* established, the toys, normally made for export, are too costly or inappropriate for local use. It is probable, for example, that a mother who spends the day making playthings for the European market cannot afford to buy her own child those, or indeed, any other toys. Perhaps harder to believe is the possibility that her and her neighbours' children have never played with a purpose-built toy of any description, much less one created with a specific educational role in mind.

Many engineers working in development see a connection between this absence of toys and the lack of mechanical sympathy often observed in developing countries. They believe that exposure to mechanical concepts at an early age, even those introduced in simplified form through toys, is crucial to understanding and sympathising with how machines work. Without this experience, the machine is too easily viewed as a 'black box' – so long as it operates effectively, it is accepted – once broken, it is abandoned or repaired to the minimum. Preventative maintenance is often an important missing piece in the puzzle of development.

This case study outlines a project undertaken by ITDG's Industrial Services Division (ITIS) to establish the production of educational pre-school toys in Sri Lanka. A teacher training programme was incorporated in the project to promote effective use of the toys. It is intended that this profile could be used as a framework for potential replication. To aid anyone trying to evaluate their own circumstances, a questionnaire is included.

Two factors, unique to the Sri Lankan setting should be made clear at the outset. Sri Lanka (population 14 million) has an unusually high literacy rate for a Third World country — 75% of the adults read and write — and a well-established state education system, instituted in 1945. ITIS's collaborating agency, the Sarvodaya Shramadana Movement, is a rural development charity which operates a network of pre-schools and plantation crêches throughout the country in the context of its Children's Services Programme. Additional pre-schools (an estimated 3,000 - 4,000) are supported by various charities, government and non-government agencies and local institutions. These 'pre-schools' may vary from a simple dirt floor shack where children are child-minded, to an established playgroup with a trained teacher, but in practically every case they will have begun as a means of caring for the families of working parents.

Interest in converting these playgroups, which include children aged 1 - 6, into pre-schools geared toward early learning is fairly recent, springing from the logical growth of the education system which has indicated a need for better preparation, more wide-spread motivation and a greater emphasis on vocational skills. With 22% of the population under the age of 6, it is of particular concern that (despite the availability of state-supported education to University level) the number of early school leavers is on the rise.

While many of these school leavers are responding to the pressure of poverty and the need to work, there are also indications that the current formal educational system does not always prepare a child for the employment requirements he will meet after school. As long as this is true, education is a luxury for most children in a country where the average annual income is £100 and a wide range of basic skills, instilled at an early age, could be a most valuable gift.

RUGBY, 1984

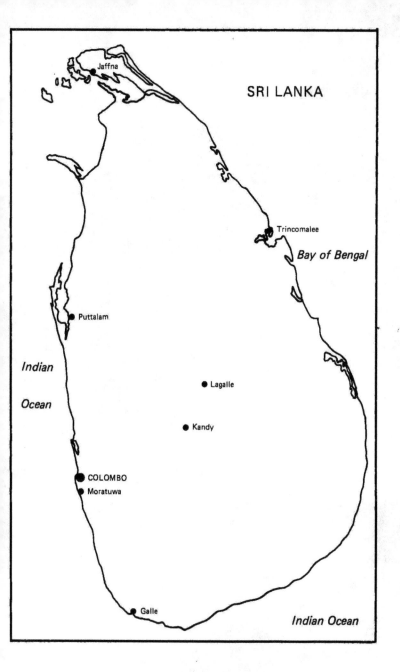

SRI LANKA

Jaffna

Trincomalee

Bay of Bengal

Puttalam

Indian

Ocean

Lagalle

Kandy

COLOMBO
Moratuwa

Galle

Indian Ocean

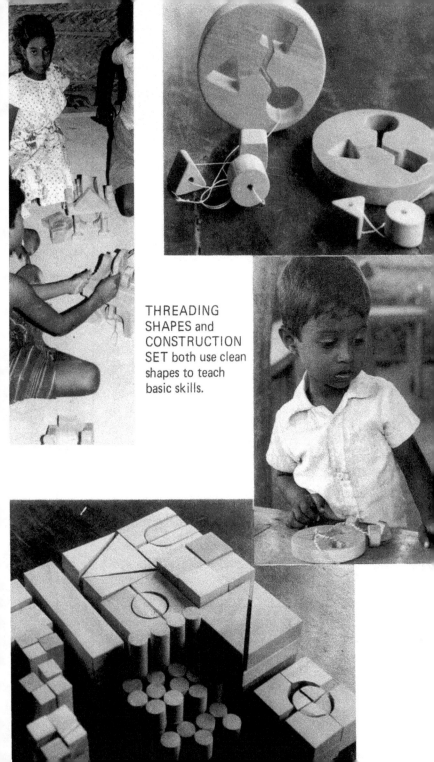

THREADING SHAPES and CONSTRUCTION SET both use clean shapes to teach basic skills.

1. A SUMMARY OF THE PROJECT

The idea of producing a range of educational toys in Sri Lanka is not new. Agencies have, in fact, been addressing themselves to the subject for a time. The questions have been . . . . what sort of toy, made of what material and by whom? By establishing this pilot ITIS/Sarvodaya project it is hoped that some of these questions can be answered.

The Sarvodaya Movement, founded in 1958, contacts about 6,000 villages through its activities which promote traditional cultural values and encourage self-help. Their 2,500 pre-schools were the stimulus and are now the primary market for the new toys.

It was through a survey of these schools that Sarvodaya first identified the lack of educational toys as a significant shortcoming. Teachers were found trying to make toys from scraps of cloth and paper, an unsatisfactory solution in a village where a discarded container is precious; and, in the short term, perhaps an impractical goal given the present available level of pre-school teacher training.

The result was a request, in 1981, from Sarvodaya for assistance in setting up local production of a range of educational toys. ITIS met this, firstly, with its own evaluation and then with the services of consultant toy designer/producer, Tim Godwin. He was sent to Sri Lanka to assess the feasibility of establishing a small woodworking unit, develop ideas for appropriate designs and evaluate local markets.

Feasibility Study

During this first consultancy visit the basic requirements for the project were established and the following recommendations were made:

1

- Markets — The potential market within Sarvodaya (currently consisting of an estimated 2,500 pre-schools with a further 3,000, or more plantation crêches) was large enough to absorb the total production of the intended 5 - 7 man workshop, but exclusively internal sales were not thought desirable. Other agencies operating pre-schools were approached and expressed interest. It was decided that half the production should be sold outside Sarvodaya as a means of increasing cash flow and helping with initial costs.

- Location — The toy unit was to be sited within one of Sarvodaya's established woodworking centres. The Moratuwa Centre was chosen, as it was the headquarters of the Movement and, also, of Sarvodaya's pre-school teacher training programme.

- Staff — Sarvodaya could staff the new unit with carpenters. Handicapped women from the centre would be included as assembly workers. The supervisor and the worker undertaking quality control were seen as vital to the project's success.

Implementation

In early 1983, having ordered the necessary machinery and completed the toy designs, Tim Godwin returned to Sri Lanka to implement the project. The second consultancy visit was scheduled to take place after the arrival of the new tools so that they could be checked. This proved to be a sensible arrangement as the base-plate of one of the machines, which had been cracked in transit, was replaced free of charge and taken out by the consultant, thus avoiding expense and delays.

The work programme, originally planned for six weeks, included:

2

Establishing the Workshop, which involved determining the production unit's physical layout, setting up the new machinery, supervising the making of jigs and templates, and establishing an administrative system for costing production flow, materials supply, marketing and sales.

Hiring and Training the Staff, which included the selection of appropriate craftsmen and administrative staff, interviewing, evaluating technical skills and creating an effective team which could operate as a separate business within the established woodworking centre. By assessing and establishing appropriate relationships between various members of staff it should be possible to insure that production flow and quality control could be maintained. Training would also be provided, as necessary.

After evaluating several pre-school operations it became clear that many of the teachers had not played with toys as children and also had little experience in the use of pre-school toys during training. They would need instruction if the project was to have any value. An extension of six weeks (funded by Oxfam) was therefore undertaken to plan and implement what became the project's third phase.

The Teacher Training Programme, which took the form of seminars and practical sessions, was designed to instruct the teachers in the educational role of each toy and to suggest ways of introducing it, focusing on special needs and emphasising the importance of evaluating each child's level of skill. The course also set out to increase the teacher's appreciation of the designs as teaching aids and to emphasise the value of gaining feedback through observation. The teachers' suggestions for design modifications and new developments would be incorporated as the toy range developed.

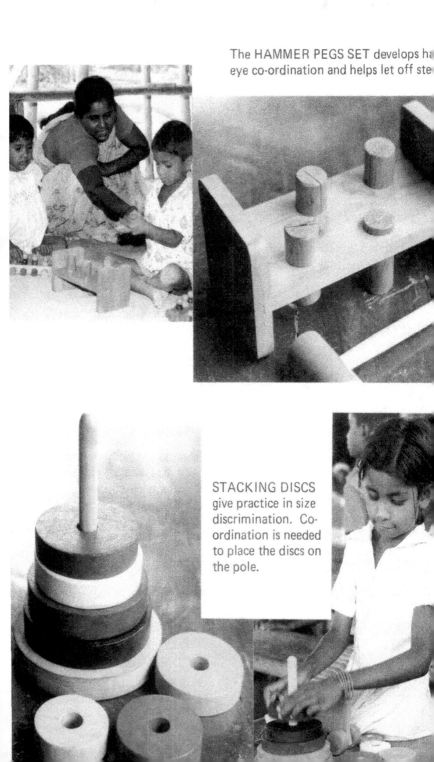

The HAMMER PEGS SET develops hand eye co-ordination and helps let off ste[am]

STACKING DISCS give practice in size discrimination. Coordination is needed to place the discs on the pole.

2. TOY DESIGNS

The 25 toys which make up the Sarvodaya/ITIS toy kit were designed by Tim Godwin for the Sri Lankan market, each with the development of certain basic skills in mind. They are intended primarily for children aged one to six but this age range is approximate and, in any case, the simplicity of most designs lends itself to imaginative play which can be enjoyed by older children.

Each toy, through the manipulation of its moving parts and/or the demands which it imposes on the child to make it 'work', is intended to stimulate a range of abilities — physical, intellectual, creative and social.

The designs are deceptively simple. For example, in the construction set, a collection of 152 bricks, various shapes are created on a 25mm module so that combinations of bricks will produce equal height and dimensions. This technique can later be used to teach mathematical concepts on the same principle as Cuisenaire Rods.

The toys utilise fundamental shape and size relationships to teach physical skills such as hand-eye co-ordination, balance and dexterity. They are also designed to stimulate a child's awareness of the laws which govern his or her environment (gravity, acceleration) and to provide opportunities to observe characteristics of objects such as spacial relationships, colour matching and ordering.

There has been particular focus on designs which stimulate imaginative play and creative activity, providing the opportunity for children to practice acting out adult roles and helping them come to terms with new experiences.

In each design, care has been taken that edges are rounded, no nails are used as fasteners (wooden axles secure the wheels, etc.) and no single part is small enough to be swallowed. Smooth wood surfaces make the toys pleasurable to grasp and touch, as well as durable and easily repaired. All paints and varnishes are non-toxic.

The toy designs are divided into five approximate age groups. Descriptions of a selection have been included.

Group A (1 to 1½ years)

1.   **Threading Shapes**. The child learns to manipulate shapes through corresponding cut-outs in a 5" wooden disc. This toy develops two-handed co-ordination, grasping, hand-eye co-ordination and basic shape identification.

2.   **Hammer Pegs**. This set gives practice in grasping, wrist control and aim.

3.   **Posting Box**. More advanced shape identification and matching can be practised and hand-eye co-ordination developed. The discovery that articles placed inside boxes are not lost is an important recognition. The four interchangeable lids allow younger children to start with simple shapes to avoid frustration. Help will be required to establish an individual's correct starting level.

4.   **Pull-A-Long Elephant**. The wheeled elephants come in sets of three – small, medium and large. These toys encourage co-ordination in walking and balance and stimulate creative play. The elephants can also be separated and pulled individually.

5.   **Sand Tools**. (spade, rake and three sand combs). The spade and rake provide practice in manual skills and co-ordinations and provide an opportunity to play out adult-associated roles. The sand combs offer a means of developing pattern making and encourage the discovery of lines and shapes created in the sand.

Group B (1½ to 2 years)

1.   **Stacking Discs**. A set of circular discs stack on a central pole, forming a pyramid shape. This develops building skills and ability in size identification which is needed to form a balanced pyramid.

2. **Peg-man Bus**. This toy encourages the development of hand-eye co-ordination and early colour matching skills. Placing the figures in the round holes provides an important step toward the development of writing skills. The peg people and vehicle stimulate imaginative and creative play.

3. **Roundabout**. A more sophisticated version of the peg-man bus concept. The platform spirals up and down a central pole, a source of fascination for children.

4. **Stand-Up Puzzles**. Comprising a set of three jig-saw animals that stand upright. They serve as an introduction to hand and eye co-ordination together with refined shape identification and matching the assembled animals may then be used as a stimulus to imaginative play and story situations.

Group C (2 to 3 years)

1. **Skittles.** Nine skittles, in three rows, form a square (corner towards the player). Each child bowls three times, the winner being the one who knocks down the most skittles. This is a helpful toy for body and eye control and co-operation with others.

2. **Twist Disc.** The player must move the disc from one end of the pole to the other. This requires refined hand-eye-wrist co-ordination. Care is needed to avoid frustration as correct manipulation is difficult.

3. **Turning Cogs.** These four cogs can be rotated to turn each other when placed in the correct sequence. This toy develops size discrimination and initial mechanical concepts.

4.   **Hobby Horse.** The largest toy in the kit, this provides practice in co-operation (two or three children may ride the horse at once), develops balance and can encourage role playing or associative play connected with adult activities.

5.   **Shapes Board.** Shapes must be matched to correct pegs, numbering 1 - 5. This toy demands shape discrimination and advanced hand-eye co-ordination.

Group D (3 to 4 years)

1.   **Threading Toys.** A weaving frame and lacing board promote early creative ability and refine hand-eye skills. Using needles and coloured cloth strips, great variation can be achieved. Sewing skills are also introduced.

2.   **Roller Colour.** Colour matching and problem solving is introduced in a game for two children. The coloured dice must be matched by a section of the roller which involves manipulation up and down a 'ladder'.

Group E (4 to 6 years)

1.   **Noughts and Crosses.** This game develops tactical skills in slightly older children who must place a nought or cross within a vacant square. The winner forms a straight line of three pieces.

2.   **Construction Set.** This set of 152 blocks helps in the further development of most skills already mentioned while encouraging co-operation and creativity. Children will have a chance to plan and build together and refine their skills of balance and co-ordination.

It is a primary consideration in all these designs to avoid frustration. The parts are sturdy and work easily; the structures are simple and leave room for invention. This opportunity for personal freedom, basic to the design concept of the toy range, is seen as the only effective answer to the proverbial challenge of the child who insists on 'throwing away the toy and playing with the box'.

3. SETTING UP THE PRODUCTION WORKSHOP

The toy production unit, sited within the Savodaya carpentry workshop, utilises an area of approximately 2,200 square feet, divided as follows:

Machine shop	900 sq ft
Office and store	300 sq ft
Spray room	200 sq ft
Assembly room and stock area	800 sq ft

Layout and Equipment

For the new toy section to operate successfully in the established general carpentry workshop, it was necessary to create an isolated work area. This prevented disturbance while working and aided in security (toys being small and novel are vulnerable to petty theft) but most importantly, it allowed the new unit to feel itself an entity and to develop its own team spirit and working codes.

Achieving this involved considerable re-arrangement of living, storage and office space and required delicate negotiations. A positive approach was needed to achieve co-operation as the toy unit's ability to create work, produce income and, eventually, hand out work to the general workshop, was argued. In fact, work was generated immediately with an order for boxes to hold the toy kits.

The layout (overleaf) was designed to facilitate the production flow. The machining section includes:

Lathe, bandsaw and jigsaw used for basic shaping; pillar drill for making holes (wheel fittings, pegmen holes, eyes, etc.); belt sander for pre-finishing and Engis head/pneumatic finishing heads for final finishing.

The installation of the electrics was part of Sarvodaya's contribution which included setting up and preparing the new unit.

9

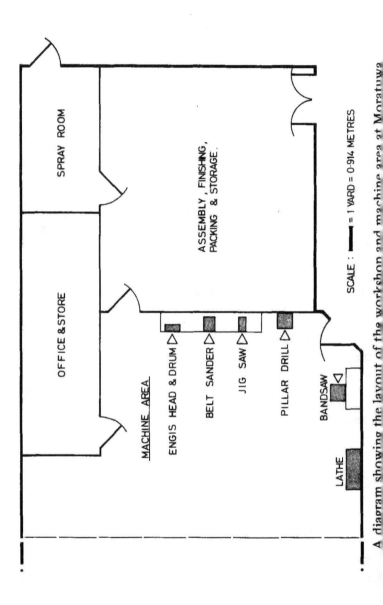

A diagram showing the layout of the workshop and machine area at Moratuwa

MACHINE AREA

ENGIS HEAD & DRUM

BELT SANDER

JIG SAW

PILLAR DRILL

BANDSAW

LATHE

OFFICE & STORE

SPRAY ROOM

ASSEMBLY, FINISHING, PACKING & STORAGE.

SCALE : ▬▬ = 1 YARD = 0.914 METRES

Although both single and three-phase electrical supply had been in use at the workshop, the internal wiring was badly worn and rewiring was necessary. While the machines used at Moratuwa required both single (220v) and three-phase supply (440v) all the equipment could have been supplied with single phase motors had it been necessary.

The Sarvodaya electrician completed the installation with two assistants, placing cables below the floor for safety and fitting all machines with earth-return trips which, should a fault occur, would isolate the machine. This prevents accidents and avoids the failure of one machine stopping total production. In wiring the spray room, precautions were taken against fire by placing all the switchgear for the new flame-proof extractor fan, light and spray gun compressor outside the room.

Although the costs of these electrical installations were a major item in the workshop expenses, they were considered essential to the safety and efficiency of the unit.

Seven new machines were provided to the project by ITIS, as follows: bandsaw, sander, jigsaw, Engis head and pneumatic finishing heads, portable dust extractor, spray gun/compressor and flame proof extractor fan, together with sufficient consumables for the two month training and start-up phase.

These were shipped from the UK, arriving with only one damaged part, as mentioned. Customs clearance charges were not imposed as the plant was to produce educational materials. Unpacking, assembly and positioning of the machines took one week, before training could begin.

An important lesson learned during this process related to the intended sharing of certain items of machinery with the carpentry workshop. It had been planned that the lathe and pillar drill would be used by both the general and the toy workshop. This proved to be possible but not optimal. The positioning and access of these important machines quickly became controversial. It was decided that they be located in the toy section but, inevitably, interruptions in production flow resulted.

Sharing equipment also proved inappropriate for the toy makers as the drill had been (mis)used for slotting and was inaccurate; and similarly, the lathe was unsuitable for precise turning. Both these machines could adversely affect production standards.

Surplus woodworking benches were utilised for the new machines and as worktops for assembly and finishing. Racking for tools, sprayed toys and storage was made to order, where needed, out of wire mesh and timber frames. Storage for timber and finished goods, although not an immediate problem, needs to be considered, long term.

The finishing equipment ran into climatic difficulties, a potential problem in any technical transfer. The spray gun, though designed to work hot, was overheating and running time had to be cut down by a half, to 15–20 minutes, before resting. The humidity during the rainy season (95% - 99%) caused some 'blooming' (whereby moisture, trapped under faster drying varnish or paint, causes it to turn milky white). Retarders (which were available locally) were suggested as a means of slowing down the drying process.

Sarvodaya's own metal workshop was given the task of making a turntable for the sprayers and this was easily done. However, they experienced difficulty in fitting the Engis head and the pneumatic sander head to the double spindle motor. Savings on both time and cost could probably have been made by contracting that part of the work to an outside firm.

A list of the machiney and equipment needed to establish the toy workshop is detailed in Appendix 1.

Raw Materials and Consumables

Two local timbers ('Kolon' and 'Panaka') were identified as the most suitable woods available. Both are "hard" woods with qualities similar to Mahogany type timbers found throughout the world. Although higher in price than other possible choices, these woods will provide overall savings due to their good machining qualities i.e., bandsaw blades will tend to last longer and sanding belts will not clog as quickly. The more unevenly grained woods, such as Teak, require greater skill in machining and more labour intensive finishing. For designs which can be painted, the visual qualities of the material are not so important and a cheaper type of timber is appropriate.

It was found that the local timber was not well seasoned, but 'movement' in the toys, after manufacture, was not a problem, as it was catered for in the original designs.

Both woods were initially purchased in rough plank form (current prices: Kolon, Rs 180 per cubic foot; Panaka, Rs 162 per cubic foot). The price for small order/planked timber is high and, once orders have grown, purchasing timber in log form to convert into planks at the workshop would allow savings. However, in Sri Lanka, as in many developing countries, the purchase of lumber in log form requires a government permit. By obtaining timber in job lots or utilising scrap off-cuts, in co-operation with a local woodworking operation, savings could also be made.

The plywood required for a few of the toy designs, i.e. the posting box and sand combs, had to be of high quality. The locally manufactured plywood was found to be unsuitable (though it proved adequate for the toy box) and an import had to be used. Solid wood was later used for the toy box and found to be cheaper.

Sources for the workshop's two primary consumables were found in Sri Lanka. Bandsaw blades (approximately one per day) were obtained in Colombo and sanding belts (two per week) were found locally. Blades for the fretsaw, though not available locally, will last a considerable time and mailing costs from the UK would be nominal.

General finishing materials were also available in Sri Lanka, in a good range of colours, but as the cost was high, care was advised with regard to the overuse of the spray gun and thickness of the coats. This was difficult to enforce as the toy makers enjoyed spraying and tended to be too enthusiastic.

Although the suppliers were unable to give a written guarantee on each individual batch of paints supplied, overall tests made by the manufacturers were confirmed in writing as conforming to the British Toy Safety Regulations and were, therefore, considered safe for use on the toys.

For more detailed information on raw materials and consumables see Appendix 1.

Staff and Training

The initial staff for the toy unit was set at seven, comprising four toy makers, to be chosen from employees of the existing Sarvodaya carpentry section, a co-ordinator, a chief finisher/collator and one assistant. In choosing the craftsmen, the primary criteria used were skill and interest. As the team took shape the best workers developed a sympathy with the toys and an enthusiasm to produce quality items.

The responsibilities of each job and the qualities sought were as follows:

In hiring the toy makers, able craftsmen were sought who, after training on all machines, would be able to use the jigs and templates to fashion and finish toys to the point of assembly. Carpenters with an eye for detail and an interest in making toys were found to be best qualified. The toy makers, once hired, began by making complete toys, as the assemblers had not yet been selected, a circumstance which probably provided the ideal introduction to the job.

Four toy makers were chosen from the original workshop staff, two of whom had helped produce trial toys during the feasibility study. These two craftsmen made headway, immediately. and found producing a quality product not only more demanding but also more satisfying than the work previously undertaken at the workshop. Two were not

14

sufficiently interested to continue and were replaced by trainees. Ideally, craftsmen chosen for such a project should also be interested in training new staff.

The key job, that of Co-ordinator, has three aspects and involves full responsibility for maintaining the workshop's daily momentum as well as a half time toy making commitment. His areas of responsibility include:

1. Personnel — maintaining motivation and discipline. His commitment to the toy project is important if he is to succeed in motivating workers to maintain production and quality control, especially if, as in a volunteer organisation, pay is low.

2. Supervising production — overseeing operational aspects in all phases, checking quality control and scheduling work.

3. Purchasing, marketing and sales — choosing sources and judging needs of consumables and raw materials within a limited budget plus stimulating both interest and sales.

The Co-ordinator chosen for Moratuwa was previously attached to the Sarvodaya Centre at Kandy. He had experience of setting up small businesses there and in the Philippines, recognised the toy unit's potential and was eager to meet the challenge. It was decided to put him in overall charge of both the toy making and the carpentry section.

The assemblers (two workers, a supervisor and an assistant) fit the toys together and, perhaps more importantly, help maintain quality control. The supervisor, ideally, returns any faulty work to the craftsmen for correction. To undertake this, and also to train and manage younger assistants, requires a person of tact and some maturity.

The original staffing choice for this job, a girl of high academic standard, proved unsuitable. Although quick to learn, she was not used to working with her hands. Also due to the social standing of women in Sri Lanka, problems arose when she referred poor work back to the male craftsmen. As a result this part of the job had to be taken over by the Co-ordinator.

During training the carpenters were taught the techniques of using the new machines with the initial work devoted to making boxes for jigs and templates. The first toy was produced within a week and most of the production training had been completed within a month.

The two Sarvodaya carpenters picked up the techniques quickly and soon produced toys of reliable quality. One, in particular, was able to contribute to the design and development of the jigs. The other, equally skillful, proved less perfectionistic and motivated. A bonus scheme was suggested as one means of stimulating interest and rewarding the staff.

Jig and template manufacture, which involved making a set of plywood templates for marking out each toy, was undertaken during the training period. Use of templates minimises wood wastage and provides significant savings, particularly in locations like Sri Lanka where the cost of wood is significantly higher than that of labour.

The templates also provide drill location holes and are marked with printed instructions as to correct drill sizes. This method is used because the workshop, lacking a planer/thicknesser, is not working with uniform sizes of timber and therefore cannot make use of conventional drilling jigs.

A custom made jig was produced to cut large discs on the bandsaw with accuracy and speed. Simple templates were also constructed to gauge the correct diameter of turnings on the lathe.

4. TOY PRODUCTION

During the first weeks of training, toys were produced in runs of 2-3 each. These were later sold, substantially minimizing material and training costs. The initial order, for 15 kits, came from Redd Barna (Norwegian Save The Children Fund), the result of their visiting the workshop.

In filling this first order, valuable experience was gained in making full use of the machinery and avoiding workshop congestion. This balancing act, which is the key to any efficient workshop, must take account of the following considerations:

1. In batch manufacturing the production time for each item, on each machine, is different. The best scheduling avoids large back-ups on any one machine. The objective is to get a balance between the time a worker is waiting and the time a machine is lying idle.

2. It is also important to schedule the cutting of designs to optimize the use of the wood sizes available.

3. Raw materials must be purchased in appropriate quantities to avoid the expense and inconvenience of holding too much inventory while ensuring uninterrupted production.

By the time the Sarvodaya toy unit had completed its first order, it was clear that constant pressure from the Co-ordinator would be required to meet delivery dates. While power cuts and miscalculations on production time were partly responsible for a slower rate of output, the absence of the consultant for a short period had also, undoubtedly, made a difference. Although market demand for the toys would help maintain pressure on the workers, in the end it must be the responsibility of the Co-ordinator to deal out the work and check that it is completed.

A general view of the workshop and machine area. The Co-ordinator (in the background) is using the belt sander while a trainee finishes a Pull-A-Long Elephant on the Engis Head.

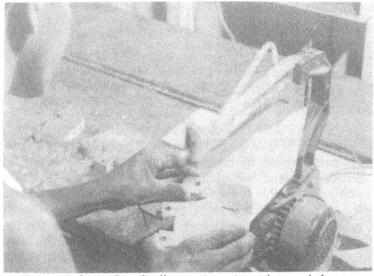

A toy maker using the jig saw to cut out internal shapes.

18

The finished toys are sprayed with varnish.

An adjustable disc-cutting jig is used on the bandsaw.

The initial rate of production was established at one toy kit per day and the consultant advised that production batches should not exceed 15 - 20 kits, i.e., 2 - 3 weeks workshop time. Larger orders should be split into smaller deliveries to avoid congestion and help maintain cash flow.

While production runs of this size could be considered small and time consuming, the priorities for a unit like the Sarvodaya workshop should be maintaining production and meeting delivery dates. It is important for the survival of a small business to avoid order cancellations both as a means of building a reliable reputation and to ensure a constant turnover of revenue.

5. MARKETS AND MARKETING

Internal Sales

The project was initiated to supply Sarvodaya's pre-schools. This market is regarded as the prime user of the educational toy kits and currently represents about 2,500 pre-schools ranging from small groups of 6 - 10 children to as many as 35 children. At the present rate of production (about one toy kit per day) the potential sales within the organisation would not be satisfied for some time, especially as the pre-school programme is expanding to include all the villages (estimated at more than 6,000) where the Movement is directly involved.

The orders from the internal Sarvodaya market originate either directly from the district centres or from the central office at Moratuwa. In either case, the confirmation and payment are centralised and the respective district's account is debited accordingly.

Sarvodaya's Plantation Workers Development Services (SSPWS) could provide a substantial increase in internal sales through its crêche programme. This organisation was set up to look after the interests of the workers on tea, rubber and coconut plantations (considered by some, to be the most underpriviliged sector of the population). The plantation crêches are less structured and educationally oriented than the pre-schools, having as their purpose childcare for working parents. Initially, therefore, only the simpler toy designs were seen as appropriate for this organisation.

Home Markets

In addition to the large Sarvodaya market, orders began to come from other groups involved in pre-school education in Sri Lanka. These sales will be an invaluable source of revenue and publicity for the toy workshop. It was agreed by the consultant and the Co-ordinator that ideally a 50-50 split between the internal and external sales should be maintained.

The groups supporting pre-school education either directly or indirectly within Sri Lanka include private voluntary organisations, government agencies and educational establishments. Enthusiastic support was shown for the new toy range, with initial and follow-up orders coming from: The Children's Secretariat (in co-operation with UNICEF), Redd Barna, the local Ladies College and Lions Club, US Save the Children, Montessori and several church-run pre-schools in rural locations as well as many individuals and some exporting organisations.

Redd Barna purchased 15 kits for field testing in various environments. The Children's Secretariat's Executive Secretary was given 3 kits for testing in selected rural, urban and government playschools. Thus, the acceptability of the new toy range to children from contrasting circumstances was soon being tested.

UNICEF, although not running any pre-schools directly, is concerned with the lack of play materials available in Sri Lanka, and is considering the purchase of toys for pre-schools throughout the country. It has been evaluating a variety of toys (including a range of educational toys imported from India) with a view to identifying those most appropriate to children from different environments and backgrounds.

Problems have arisen as in the case of the Indian toys, which were to be used as model designs. These were, however, copies of sophisticated European products and their appropriateness for Sri Lankan children, particularly those in rural and plantation districts, was questionable.

A committee, representing groups connected with pre-school education in Sri Lanka, was appointed by UNICEF to evaluate how to proceed on the pre-school toy issue. The Sarvodaya toy kit, when presented to the full committee, was well received but few orders were given. The majority of the members would need UNICEF's help to purchase the toy kits in quantity, but some have placed small orders and recommended the toy range to non-members, which resulted in further sales.

Sarvodaya's Plantation Workers Development Service (SSPWS) has received UNICEF's support for a proposed workshop at Sarvodaya's Kandy Centre. This second toy unit would meet the needs of the plantation children, a market which involves 700 plantations, each operating 3 to 7 crêches, possibly as many as 3,000 – 4,000 in all.

The head of SSPWS, initially, expressed interest in the new toy range and purchased several kits but believed many of the designs were too sophisticated for the plantation children. She contended that due to poor nutrition, these children are 2 - 3 years behind their urban counterparts. The new toy production unit will probably produce only the simpler designs from the range. Tim Godwin prepared a feasibility study for this undertaking which was submitted to UNICEF.

Exports

As the Moratuwa workshop was established primarily to supply local markets, export sales are seen as an additional outlet which should be considered only after a strong home market has been established. When the workshop is running profitably exports would be looked at as possible 'icing on the cake'.

However, the more stringent demands of the export market for high quality and adherence to delivery dates need to be considered, as well as the potential for complications. These could include time delays (3 months minimum) between production and delivery which can put a great strain on cash flow. In addition, unforseen difficulties at customs or clearance or even displeasure with product quality upon delivery can result in non payment.

Agencies specialising in Third World trade such as Oxfam and Traidcraft, are sensitive to these problems and more likely to make allowances. Any involvement of the Sarvodaya workshop in the export market should undoubtedly be through such private voluntary organisations. The product buyer for Oxfam Bridge, Oxfam's trading group, visited the toy workshop and requested samples; NOVIB (Holland), one of Sarvodaya's major overseas aid contributors, has also expressed interest.

In a strictly commercial export exercise, current production costs, however, probably mean that the toys are overpriced for the export market at this early stage. It is important to remember that success in the export market depends on the base price of the potential product being reasonable conventional percentage add-ons at the various necessary stages can increase the price of an item, as follows:

```
For an Ex-factory price of. . . . . . . . . . . . . . . . . . . £1.00
Add 35% to cover freight & insurance. . . . . . . . . . . 0.35
                                            ─────
                                     Total £1.35

Add importer's mark–up (normally 100%). . . . . . . 1.35
                                            ─────
                                     Total £2.70
Add retail shop mark–up (normally 100%)  . . . . . . 2.70
                                            ─────
                                     Total £5.40
Add on Value Added Tax 15% . . . . . . . . . . . . . . . . . .81
                                            ─────
                    Selling Price to Public  Total £6.21
```

Although Oxfam and Tradecrafts' mark-up is less than this because they act as their own importers, the implications of this export mark-up for a new business where efficiency and quality are still being perfected can be disastrous. For every unit increase in costs through inefficiency the export price to cover this must be multiplied by a factor of 6 – as compared with a factor of two (or even less) for local markets.

At the early stages of establishing a business it is unwise to reduce prices to compensate for inefficiency. Export orders can also embarrass the production capacity of a new operation. It is wiser to wait until improved production creates a larger profit margin, thus, allowing the business to offer discounts on bulk export orders. By turning down orders that would be difficult or costly to meet, future good-will can be preserved.

One way of entering the export market would be to reduce unit costs by increasing productivity, possibly through careful collaboration with an outside workshop. It would be beneficial if this collaborator had export experience.

In order to publicise the Sarvodaya Toy Workshop, a press release was sent to all the major Sri Lankan newspapers. A 3 minute video film was also made, showing the toys and production at the workshop. This was broadcast on the television news and, together with editorial coverage, resulted in interest and sales.

6. FINANCIAL CONSIDERATIONS

*Note: At the time of writing 35 Sri Lankan Rupees (Rs)
= £1 Sterling; 24 Rs = US$1.*

Capital Costs

Total expenditure on investment in machinery, building
alterations and working capital for the Sarvodaya Toy Workshop amounted to Rs 132,180 (£3,780). Of this, approximately a third was provided by Sarvodaya to cover local costs
while two-thirds was funded by ITIS for the import of machinery. The technical assistance, provided by ITIS, cost a
further Rs 240,710 (£6,880). Details of capital expenditure
are presented in Appendix 2.

Production Costs

The workshop achieved an average production rate of one set
of 25 toys a day, employing four full time and one part time
worker. This is in accordance with the initial estimate of 20
man hours required for each set, after allowing for power
cuts, breaks and unproductive labour time. The costs of
production could therefore be calculated on a daily basis and
were estimated to be Rs 580 a day (or per set of toys). See
Appendix 3 for details.

It is expected that with more experience, the rate of
output can be improved bringing a consequent reduction in
the cost of the toy sets. At a rate of one set per day, when
total costs are Rs 580 per set, labour costs amount to Rs5
per productive hour, while actual pay is about Rs 2.60 per
hour. There is, therefore, a margin for bonus payments to
the workers as an incentive for higher productivity. Although
not usual practice within Sarvodaya, the introduction of
bonus payments might also serve to retain the workers whose
skills have been increased, by bringing their income up to
about Rs 800 per month, the going rate for good wood-
workers in the Moratuwa district.

26

Although Sarvodaya agreed that the bonus system would be a good idea, they saw it operating on a half yearly basis to coincide with the toy section's accounting procedures. It was recommended that, if bonus payments were paid quarterly, workers could see a more immediate return for their labours. Payment to the toy makers from profits generated by increased productivity would undoubtedly have substantial long term benefit to the project.

A large proportion of the production costs were accounted for by direct or variable costs, principally new materials. Unnecessary wastage in the use of materials or changes in prices could, therefore, be significant for the viability of the workshop. In order to monitor these costs for each toy (raw materials, labour, consumables) a system for keeping cost records was established, thus enabling a continuous check to be maintained on the direct costs of production.

Projections and Profitability

Assuming 264 working days a year, the annual output of the workshop would be at least 264 sets of toys, with an annual turnover of approximately Rs 184,000. This would yield a net profit of Rs 35,000 from which purchases of additional equipment might be made.

The potential market, with several thousand pre-schools and crêches in Sri Lanka, is more than capable of absorbing the output of the Sarvodaya workshop. Rapid expansion to meet this demand could, however, cause problems with product quality and the ability to meet orders. It was recommended, therefore, that any expansion should be implemented gradually, allowing sufficient time for training workers and for building up the necessary financial resources.

7. THE PRE-SCHOOL TEACHER TRAINING PROGRAMME

One-day training seminars were organised at the Sarvodaya and Redd Barna pre-schools to introduce the toy range to the teachers. The programme focused on the educational purpose of each design, its approximate age range/skill levels and ways in which the same toy might be used to stimulate children of different age groups. Guidance was given on introducing complex toys to very able children and simpler designs to those of less ability with the emphasis on evaluating the individual's skill level.

Programme Outline

The Sarvodaya teacher training course took place at Moratuwa where the pre-school, which is attended by 35 children, doubles as a training centre for teachers from Sarvodaya's other centres and villages.

These seminars began with an introduction and explanation of the toy range, followed by practical play with the children and demonstrations on fabricating play items from scrap material. The seminars were very well attended and the teachers were enthusiastic.

The subtlety of how children learn through play was illustrated most effectively in practical demonstration. For example, it is important that the child (not the teacher) dismantles the stacking discs if he or she is to learn the technique of re-assembling them.

It was stressed that the toys had not been provided to make the pre-school teachers' job easier by keeping the children entertained. In fact, to gain maximum benefit from each toy, the teacher would have to be more aware of each child's abilities and frustrations without being over-attentive and stifling creativity. The point was made that it is when a child enjoys playing that learning follows most naturally.

The teachers also visited the workshop to gain an understanding of the capabilities of the producers, an insight which should help them provide relevant suggestions for the development of new designs. This process began immediately when children had difficulty working the animal jigsaws and it was suggested that one side of the puzzles be painted to make reassembly easier.

The teacher training course is seen as a vital ingredient in the successful duplication of this project. In Sri Lanka, it happened that the current head of Sarvodaya's pre-school programme, an individual already committed to the concept of early education, was able to continue these seminars. Under different circumstances it would be necessary to find an appropriate person for this essential function.

A similar course was carried out at five pre-schools within Redd Barna's resettlement programme. This programme undertakes to provide homes and livelihoods to numbers of homeless families in a variety of locations including urban slums, fishing villages, rural areas and plantation districts. Despite the contrast between these environments, little difference was observed in the abilities of the children to relate to the toys.

Evaluation of Toys During Practical Play Sessions

During these training sessions, a preference for certain toys emerged. The pull-along elephant, construction set, hobby horse, peg-man bus and the stacking discs were most popular – all toys which can be played with by more than one child at a time. The other designs were well received with the exception of noughts and crosses and roller colour. These games, which require more guidance, will probably be taken up once the novelty of the range has worn off and teachers have more time. However, their acceptance will be monitored.

Frequently, the children invented original ways of using toys such as towing the peg bus behind an elephant or turning the hobby horse into a wheelbarrow to carry bricks. This kind of creativity is an important aspect of play which represents the first steps toward independent thinking and problem solving.

Making Toys from Scrap

There is a school of thought in Sri Lanka which suggests that it should be possible for pre-school teachers to improvise and produce useful pre-school toys from local waste materials. This is arguable, however, within the current situation in that pre-schools exist primarily as a financial consideration, their main purpose being to free the adults in a family to work and earn an income.

Traditionally, therefore, young girls are employed who, until now, have seen their role as one of childminder. Until this emphasis changes, it is unreasonable to expect innovation from them to create effective toy designs and purpose built toys are probably the only realistic alternative.

While more qualified teachers will undoubtedly be capable of making toys, the cost and availability of scrap (in both urban and rural areas) and time constraints, will make the task difficult. At present, most pre-school teachers and assistants are kept very busy indeed just seeing to the needs of the children, keeping things tidy and preparing the meal or refreshments as necessary.

8. SIX MONTHS ON – A FOLLOW-UP VISIT

Tim Godwin returned to Moratuwa to evaluate the project's progress after the toy unit had been in operation for six months (March - October, 1983). He found that:

• The original staff remained with the exception of one trainee who had left (for better wages) and had been replaced by two new men; so the workers now totalled 5, plus the Co-ordinator. Quality was being maintained by the carpenters but the quality control was still under the supervision of the Co-ordinator.

• The prices of the primary raw materials (Panaka and Kolon) were continuing to rise and it had been decided to purchase a less expensive timber for those toys which were coloured or painted.

• Orders were increasing for the general carpentry work-shop which was seen as beneficial to the toy unit. Woodplex, a local manufacturer of knock-down wooden furniture for export, was ordering quantities of small items (cheeseboards, kitchen utensils, small tables, trays, lamps, etc.) made with off-cuts from their furniture operation.
These products were being sold to the local market. Some off-cuts could also be used to provide savings for the toy workshop.

• It had become obvious that the long term success of the toy unit, operating as a business within a business, would benefit from the strengthening of the general workshop. Woodplex's owner could give up to Rs 50,000 of work per month to the general carpentry workshop at such time as it could handle that workload. He plans to lend the workshop one of his top carpenters and some pieces of redundant machinery to help fill these orders. Seven new workers were being taken on to fill Woodplex's orders.

• The new work subcontracted from Woodplex will require an increase of 5 - 10 workers in a new assembly and finishing

31

section which will service both the general and toy workshops. The new staff will include handicapped girls from the Sarvodaya centre, as previously intended.

It was necessary to find solutions to some difficulties which had developed during the Sarvodaya/ITIS Workshop's first six months of production. In this period, Rs 47,500 worth of goods had been manufactured with a net loss of Rs 5,500, compared with the projected figures which anticipated a profit of Rs 11,000. The cause of this was lost production time which had increased the labour costs of each toy kit produced to 3 times higher than budgeted.

The reasons for this production shortfall were identified and problems resolved:

- Working conditions and power supplies, disrupted during the civil disturbances, had returned to normal. However, in that period, mid-July/mid-August production had halted for 2 - 3 weeks and the consequent absenteeism had totalled 54 days over the six months, all of which had a distorting effect on the total financial picture.

- The workshop had run into difficulties obtaining band saw blades when the local supplier stopped production. Woodplex was able, however, to identify a source of Korean-made blades and arrangements were made for them to supply the workshop's needs.

- Production had also suffered from interruptions by the general carpentry section. This inevitable conflict, caused partly by the stress of sharing equipment and partly by the difference in work loads, was being resolved with the increased orders and staffing changes stimulated by Woodplex's involvement.

The TURNING COGS will not rotate until they are in the correct sequence.

POSTING BOX
ow) develops
e identification
matching skills.
interchangeable
provide variety
challenge.

The Children pictured are from village pre-schools in Puttalam, Laggalle and Visva Madu.

It is encouraging to note that during the first three months of the toy unit's production a slight profit was shown. Although this became a loss over the six months period, problems had eased and the workshop should be able to pick up and continue its initial success.

During a later visit by ITIS staff, the results of these solutions could be seen. The carpentry section was employing 10 wood-workers, mainly new trainees, working on a steady flow of orders.

Marketing and Future Sales

Early customers continued to order the toys together with additional orders from new customers including UK Save the Children Fund, Lanka Mahila Samithi (a women's group which maintains about 100 pre-schools) a number of church groups and Montessori pre-schools. Sales to Sarvodaya also continued steadily.

The toys were being sold both in kits and individually which provided the opportunity to get some indication of which designs were selling well. Sales records showed that the peg-man bus, the stand-up puzzle, the stacking discs and the shapes board were top sellers. The spade proved to be the most popular toy in the range which was a surprise, as it is not a tool commonly used in Sri Lanka. The construction set also sold well, despite its relatively high cost.

Following discussions with buyers, modifications were made to the range. Breakages had been experienced due to rough play and skimping on materials (using thinner dowlings to achieve savings, etc.). It was suggested that more colour be used in some designs. The consultant enlarged and/or strengthened some toys and added colour where it was appropriate, for example, by colouring the shapes board (triangles became red, circles became yellow, etc.) Colour identification then becomes another aspect of the toy's function.

Requests for new designs included toys with sound or texture, a dolls house, counting toys and alphabet shapes, plus a strong box for toy storage.

Since the consultant's last visit, the overall direction of UNICEF's plans had taken shape. These include compiling a directory of Sri Lankan pre-schools, establishing 4 - 5 workshops in various locations (linked with pre-schools) and producing a large group of toy designs which will include the ITIS/Sarvodaya range. The intention is to observe the toys in use in the pre-schools and then utilise the information gathered to modify the range.

A major part of UNICEF's concept, as mentioned, involves the teachers making educational toys. While this could be difficult to achieve in present circumstances UNICEF indicated that they intend to devote a substantial part of the programme to the training and education of teachers.

The Children's Secretariat reported positively on the toy kits but found their teachers unwilling to let children use the toys during free play, fearing breakage. This problem should ease with familiarity and the recognition that the toys can be mended easily.

The Co-ordinator for Sarvodaya's pre-school programme indicated that a current effort to expand its children's health programme to include 40 additional villages will involve establishing new pre-schools. It is intended to equip these schools with toy kits.

The government's State Plantations Corporation (SPC) informed the consultant that the Sarvodaya/ITIS toy kit had been accepted as suitable for the plantation crèches. This represents a change of view as, previously, the range was considered too advanced. SPC runs the second largest group of playschools in the country.

Efforts to obtain publicity, a function which can now form a major part in the selling strategy of the toy workshop, for external sales, will include making a 20 minute video documentary on the toy production unit for television. Sarvodaya owns video production equipment, as communications is one of their primary means of promoting the Movement. Although private televisions are unusual in Sri Lanka many screens have been installed in public places and are accessible to people living in urban areas so this would be a useful means of promoting the toy range.

REPLICATION

While Sarvodaya established this toy programme to supply much-needed play equipment for its own pre-schools, the enthusiasm shown by visiting organisations concerned with pre-school education in Sri Lanka and other developing countries, suggests that there is a common need for simple educational play materials for the under-sixes. This first toy production unit has demonstrated that, for a relatively small investment, a workshop can be set up to meet this demand.

Among representatives visiting Sarvodaya, many were keen to buy the toys but several also expressed interest in replicating the workshop in Sri Lanka and other countries. In Colombo, U.S. Save the Children is setting up a wooden toy production unit which will be modelled on the Sarvodaya workshop. The ITIS consultant advised this project during his last visit to Colombo. UNICEF also plans to establish 4 - 5 similar toy workshops in various Sri Lankan locations. The proposed unit for the Sarvodaya Plantation Workers in Kandy, will be the first of these.

Among the groups planning replication abroad, the Church of South India (CSI) proposes setting up several toy making operations to supply 26,000 pre-schools throughout Southern India. Tim Godwin visited CSI in India to advise them on the feasibility of such a programme which is planned to start in 1984.

Interested parties in Malawi and Zimbabwe are also discussing replication of the Sarvodaya project. A feasibility study done with a view to setting up a production workshop in Malawi, originally concentrated on the export potential of such a project. As a result of the Sarvodaya exercise, Malawi have more recently requested that the study be restructured to focus on the local market.

The contributing factors that enabled the programme to be established successfully in Sri Lanka — a definite market, the availability of raw materials, local skills and workshop space, plus, the willingness and co-operation to implement the programme — are by no means unique. There is no reason

PULL-ALONG ELEPHANT
comes in sets of large, medium and
small. This toy gives practice in size
discrimination and develops balance.

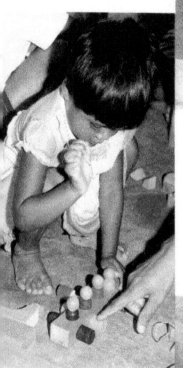

The PEG-MAN BUS helps to develop
hand-eye co-ordination. The precision
needed to place the figures, correctly,
represents an early step toward writing
skills.

The simplicity of these designs allows
a range of imaginative play for older
children.

why many countries could not replicate the project.

Furthermore, by having control over production, it is possible to modify the toy designs and introduce new items to answer the specific development needs of children in various parts of the world. The versatility of the workshop also enables the fabrication of complementary wooden items such as kitchen utensils, giftware and wooden accessories for industry which would provide additional income.

Assuming that the original Sri Lankan workshop soon begins to return sufficient profit for reinvestment, expansion of the toy programme could take the form of an enlarged workshop, or ideally, would involve setting up additional small workshops close to rural markets. Despite all economic considerations, however, it is essential to recognise that the major beneficiaries of this project will be the children. Improving the skills and stimulating the intellect of future generations is surely one of the most direct and effective ways of helping Third World countries to realize their own potential.

APPENDIX 1

Machinery and Equipment Used in Establishing the Workshop

1. Capital Equipment

1 Startrite 14" 352 bandsaw 3 phase.
1 43" x 6" RJH bench type belt sanding machine: 3 phase
1 8" x 4" Engis head
1 Pneumatic head 3" diameter
1 Special motor for Engis and drum, double ended exit spindles, single phase
1 No-volt release starter for above
1 Startrite 55 portable dust extractor, single phase
6 8" quick action clamps
1 Flameproof fan for spray room fume extraction
1 No-volt release starter for above
1 Set Leitz type 111 SP drill: 4mm–10mm (x 1mm): 14mm and 16mm
1 Leitz type 87: 18mm and 20mm twist drills
1 Leitz type 185 expanding machine bit SP. 25mm–50mm, adjustable – 140mm O/All
1 Set Leitz cutter for above   (1 large + 1 small) 185 expanding machine bit
1 Volumair T2D spray gun kit, single phase
1 Multicut 2 universal saw 230 v 50M2
4 Blade clamp 0.7mm slot for above
10 Replacement Clamp screws for above
2 Replacement knobs for above
2 Hardened steel Allen keys for above

Note: Two primary pieces of equipment, the pillar drill and the lathe are not included in this list as they were shared with Sarvodaya's General Workshop in the Moratuwa project.

2. **Consumables** (materials needed for the two month start-up phase)

15 ¼" blades for Startrite bandsaw,, 6 teeth per inch skip
 5 ½" blades as above, 6 teeth per inch skip
10 43"x 6" sanding belts for RJH bench type sanding machine: 60 grit
20 Sanding belts as above: 80 grit
 3 120 grit loadings for Engis head
 2 80 grit loadings as above
 3 Spare sets of brushes for Engis head
20 80 grit belts for pneumatic head
 6 Face masks
 3 Pairs protective glasses
 3 Packets of refills for masks (25 per packet)
 ¼ Gross no. 5 Goldsnail blades for Multicut saw
 ½ Gross each of: No 5 and No 9 Pebeco Gottfried blades as above

3. **Specifications for Surface Finishes**

Non-toxic paints — Duco Nitrocellulose basic colour 030 range of of 22 colours conformed with British toy safety regulations (1974)

Varnish & sealing — Duco Cellulose sanding sealer Conc. K008-522

Glossy finish (natural) — Duco wood finish glossy lacquer K004–182

Glue — Standard P.V.A. glue worked well with all woods used.

APPENDIX 2

Note: At the time of writing, December '83, 35 Sri Lankan Rupees (Rs) = £1 Sterling); 24 Rs = US$1.

Actual expenditure on investment for the Sarvodaya Toy Workshop amounted to Rs 132,180, the imported component (funded by ITIS) being Rs 91,560 (or 69%). In addition, land and workshop space (200 m²) were provided without charge to the project by Sarvodaya, although there was expenditure on alterations to the building.

Details of capital expenditure are as follows:

Repairs and alteration to building	Rs	3,840
Electrical fittings and installation	Rs	14,570
Workshop machinery:		
Imported CIF Colombo	Rs	81,410
Locally purchased	Rs	9,000
Machinery installation	Rs	6,210
Working capital:		
Raw materials	Rs	7,000
Consumables (imported CIF)	Rs	10,150
TOTAL	Rs	132,180

The technical assistance provided by ITIS to Sarvodaya, including fees, travel and other costs, amounted to £6,650 (Rs 232,750). Accommodation and food provided to the consultant during his 12 week stay in Sri Lanka cost Sarvodaya a total of Rs 7,960. Thus, the total cost of the technical assistance was Rs 240,710.

APPENDIX 3

Operating Costs

The Sarvodaya Workshop achieved a production rate of one set of 25 toys a day, on average. Although with more experience this rate of output can be expected to improve, the operation or production costs detailed below are based on a daily output of one set. Direct costs, other than power, are based on actual expenditure. Power and indirect costs are estimated in order to give a more accurate picture of total costs than might be obtained from the 25% of revenue taken by Sarvodaya to cover overheads.

Power cuts on the grid are a recurring problem and allowances for resulting losses in production time were made in costing the toys.

Costs per set of toys are estimated as follows:

Direct Costs per set

Wood:

Kolon, 0.5 cu. ft. @ Rs 180/cu. ft.	Rs	90
Panaka, 0.25 cu. ft. @ Rs 162/cu. ft.	Rs	40
Plywood, 0.75/sheet (24" x 16") @		
Rs 12/sheet Rs 12/sheet	Rs	8
Toy box	Rs	23

Finishes:

Varnish 1 litre @ Rs 53/litre		
(50% thinner, 50% sealer)	Rs	53
Paint, 0.1 litre @ Rs 98/litre	Rs	10

Consumables:

1 bandsaw blade and 1/3 sanding belt	Rs	69

Labour:

4.5 man days at average Rs 23.11/day	Rs	104

Power:

Estimated 8kWh @ Rs 1.26/kWh	Rs	10
TOTAL DIRECT COSTS per set	Rs	407

Indirect Costs per set

Administration:
    Half Co-ordinator's salary @ Rs 42/day   Rs   21
    Other staff (Sarvodaya Headquarters)   Rs   27
    Materials (phone, stationery, etc)   Rs   30

Maintenance:
    5% p.a. capital cost (264 days p.a.)   Rs   25

Depreciation:
    20% p.a. on equipment costs   Rs   70
    5% p.a. on building   N/A

         TOTAL INDIRECT COSTS   Rs   173
         (based on one set/day)

         TOTAL COSTS PER KIT   Rs   580

Annual Production costs: Rs 153120 (264 sets/year)

A profit margin was added to finance the business expansion discussed in this publication.

APPENDIX 4

Costs Check List

To assist those who, after reading about Sarvodaya's pre-school Toy Workshop, might be interested in establishing their own workshop, we include a check list of essential inputs for setting up and running a similar operation. Space is provided for you to note local prices and wages and thus arrive at preliminary cost estimates for investment and production.

The viability of any toy workshop, given that the necessary inputs are available, will depend on whether sets of toys can be sold at a price that will achieve a profit. An investigation of the likely market, institutional and public, is therefore advisable once cost estimates are known.

Capital Costs

Land: 500 sq. m. @ . . . . /sq. m.
    (if purchased) . . . .
Building: (200 sq. m.)
    Construction . . . .
    Electrical wiring and fitting . . . .
    Electrical connection (machinery
    rated at 5kW) . . . .
Machinery (as per Appendix 1) . . . .
Machinery installation . . . .
Furniture and fittings (work benches etc.) . . . .
Working capital(say 2 months variable costs) . . . .
Contingency 10% . . . .

        Total estimated capital cost

Operating costs (to produce one set of toys per day)

Variable costs: (A)
    Wood: 0.75 cu. ft. @. . . . ./cu.ft. . . . .
    Plywood: 2.7 sq. ft. @. . . . . ./sq.ft. . . . .
    Toy box: . . . .
    Varnish: 1 litre @. . . . ./litre . . . .
    Paint: 0.1 litre @ . . . ./litre . . . .
    * Bandsaw blade   . . . .
    * Sanding Belt   . . . .
    * Labour   . . . .
    * Power   . . . .

                  Total daily variable costs:

Fixed costs: (B)
    Rent per day (if land is not purchased) . . . .
    Administration and marketing
              Staff: 1.5 man days
                     @ . . . ./day . . . .
              Office consumables   . . . .
Maintenance:
    Building 3% p.a. of capital   . . . .
    Machinery 5% p.a. of capital   . . . .
    (for daily cost divide by 264)
Depreciation:
    Building (5% p.a.)   . . . .
    Machinery (20% p.a.)   . . . .
    (for daily cost divide by 264)

                  Total daily fixed costs

TOTAL ESTIMATED COST PER SET = A + B

Note: These elements will depend upon the productivity of local labour
       and quality of available consumable materials. As a guide, in a
       high productivity workshop, output could be expected to reach
       1½ to 2 sets of toys/day.

Printed in the USA
CPSIA information can be obtained
at www.ICGtesting.com
JSHW012057140824
68134JS00035B/3488

9 781853 390531